This is a traveler's tale,
meant to awaken the way within,
showing the true purpose of the life journey
is far more than a mere traveling to survive.
Here is your invitation to
leap at life's opportunities
as shown through the heroic actions
and revealing insights of one
Ping the frog.

Zentrepreneur Guides®
by Stuart Avery Gold and Ron Rubin

Success at Life: How to Catch and Live Your Dream

Dragon Spirit: How to Self-Market Your Dream

Tiger Heart, Tiger Mind: How to Empower Your Dream

Wowisms: Words of Wisdom for Dreamers and Doers

The Zentrepreneur's Idea Log & Workbook

ping

A Frog in Search of a New Pond

STUART AVERY GOLD

Newmarket Press

New York

This book is published in the United States of America.

ISBN 1-55704-682-4

10 9 8 7 6 5 4 3 2

Library of Congress Cataloging-in-Publication Data
Gold, Stuart Avery.
  Ping : a frog in search of a new pond / Stuart Avery Gold ;
  —1st ed.
    p. cm.
ISBN 1-55704-682-4 (cloth : alk. paper)
1. Change (Psychology) 2. Adaptability (Psychology)   I. Title.
  BF637.C4G645 2005
158′.1—dc22

                              2005021001

QUANTITY PURCHASES

Companies, professional groups, clubs, and other organizations may qualify for special terms when ordering quantities of this title. For information, write Special Sales Department, Newmarket Press, 18 East 48th Street, New York, NY 10017; call (212) 832-3575; fax (212) 832-3629; or e-mail info@newmarketpress.com.

www.newmarketpress.com

www.pingthebook.com

Illustrations by Machiko

Designed by Kevin McGuinness

Manufactured in the United States of America

This book has been printed on acid-free paper.

CONTENTS

For my two glorious leapers,
Aaryn and Shaun

Prologue

What matters is that you believe the following tale is true.

Personally, back at the beginning I had my doubts. And who wouldn't have some doubts when they first find out that the adventures described in these pages are, in point of fact, the transformative journey belonging to one of the pond's most enduring creatures . . . a frog.

Now for those of you who have just rolled your eyes, please don't be put off—there is so much to learn. Despite the many bad things going on here on planet Earth, there are many good things happening too. And one of them is that there are still stories that can thrill the spirit and soar the soul.

This is one of those stories.

Long before you and long before me, long before there was the quicksilver of WiFi, broadband, streaming video, DVD, and VCR, long before there was television, movies, radio, and even books, there were stories that entertained, educated, motivated, and inspired. And while some stories passed down through the centuries were meant to soothe and calm and perhaps put the listener to sleep, this is a traveler's tale, meant to awaken the way within, showing the true purpose of the life journey is far more than a mere traveling to survive. Here is your invitation to leap at life's opportunities as shown through the heroic actions and revealing insights of one Ping the frog.

To verify this story I interviewed dozens of people, Asians and Westerners, Tibetan lamas and Zen masters, Burmese teachers and Taoist practitioners, cramming notebooks full before setting ink to paper. Some of the interviews took me to Japan, and some to China, and some to certain sages here in the United States. But alas, only a few knew Ping's remarkable tale, and fewer still could recount it from beginning to end. After all, this took place some time ago.

But the story still haunted me and I was still hopeful, so I spent many more months conducting research until, finally, blessedly, I was able to nail down an accurate record of the facts, which is how I can come to you vouching for this story's authenticity. And whether any of my efforts were worth it, is, of course, up to you to decide. After all, if history has taught us anything, it's that some stories are for telling. And some stories are for believing.

And the story of Ping the frog?

Well, that is a story forever. . . .

1

Leap of Faith

The most meaningful journey to take is the one within.

Once upon a place . . .

The pond was not deep that day. Indeed it had been shallow for some time. But most of the pond dwellers didn't mind—it was just the way things were.

For instance, the turtles were quite happy as long as they had water enough to swim around in. They even liked to bask their shells in the sun as they topped the surface, with the water being just so. Great for the cranes, too. They liked how the shallow water made it easy to bob in for something tasty. The fish didn't complain either—being closer to the surface made it easier to seize a floating munchie.

Truth to tell, for the inhabitants of the pond, there was contentment enough to go around, never a grumble or a whisper of complaint. Most took to spending average days living out average lives without too much moodiness.

Most, but not all.

Ping was a frog, but more than that, he was a frog with a proud heritage, even though he had no memory of it. He didn't know, for example, that the ancients in China believed that frogs came from the moon, hatching from eggs that fell from the sky with the silver rain. Oh, he could go hiking back in his own time, remembering his earliest days at the pond, before he had arms and before he had legs, remembering what it was like to joyously zoom through the deep water, propelled by his tail.

And when he was older and there was jumping to be done, nothing pleased him more. Ping was an incredibly gifted jumper, the best at going the distance.

In one hop, Ping perfectly sailed nine feet—correction, sorry—nine feet three inches, an unbeatable record. Such was the remarkable talent of Ping the frog that all the denizens of the pond would stop whatever they were doing to watch when Ping jumped. They felt privileged to witness such glory.

Ping thought nothing of it. All he knew was that jumping great distances was terrific fun and that now, sadness of sadness, there was no good jumping at the pond anymore. Not with the water nearly gone.

Which brings us to the point that in order to live a life of grace beyond gravity you have to have two things. First, you have to have a strong desire to live your best life, and second, you have to have the will and willingness to live it each and every day.

Ping had both.

What he didn't have was water. And Ping needed water to jump in.

I should add, at this point, that the pond had always been spring-fed, and while doing my research, I couldn't find any clues as to

*Who can guess that precise moment
when your world is going to change?*

what had changed the course of the spring. What I did find was that while staying half-heartedly in the same old spot was fine for others, it was not at all fine for Ping.

Ping shrugged and sighed. He longed for the breadth and the depth of the once-upon-a-time deep water. He had taken such pleasure in the way the heavenly hues and intoxicating scents of the lotus and lily blossoms used to rule the water's surface. And who could argue with the serene rhythm of the reeds as they swayed along with the bamboo breezes. This waterscape had brought such happiness to his inner mind. But gone now it was, and what remained in its place did nothing for Ping's soul.

The ancient Taoist Chuang Tzu wrote, "Let everything be allowed to do what it naturally does, so that its nature will be satisfied."

Now obviously amphibians can't read, but when you're a frog, what you do and see every day shows you that all living things have a place in the natural order of things and that each has its own destiny to fulfill.

Ping sensed, no, he knew without any doubt in his heart, that what he wanted more than anything else was to live a life that would enable him to be one with what he was.

So strong was Ping's belief in his inborn talents and unique capabilities that he spent his days sitting at the pond's edge just dreaming the biggest dreams of becoming his own best self. But alas, while Ping's dreams got bigger, the pond got smaller, until that startling day when the pond was no longer a pond at all, and the comfy-cozy, safe surroundings that Ping had for so long enjoyed were going ... going ... pffft ... gone.

Nothing left.

That's an exaggeration, of course. There were twigs and stones and hapless bones, all sorts of things left behind, in the pond bed. And there was the mud. Much mud everywhere.

For days the mud was where Ping sat, and for nights the mud was where Ping slept. But he didn't sleep much. It's hard to let go when fear lurks inside you. And Ping was afraid.

Very.

Change—real change—is unsettling. When change happens, it can create the kind of fear that can take hold of even the most confident of frogs. It can instill confusion, hesitation, anger, anxiety, and desperation. Fear of change can grip and grab and seize you with such strength, it can paralyze you.

But only if you let it.

Fear of change, fear of taking risks, fear of ridicule or that someone will disapprove of your goals and dreams—these are the enemies of intention and transformation. But even enemies have enemies, and the enemy of fear is found in courage. Courage is not the absence of fear; it is acting in spite of fear.

For some, the realization of this simple fact takes time. For many the realization never comes at all. For Ping, it pretty much took about a week.

Day after day, Ping experienced emotions he'd never felt before. He was confused and uncertain.

*It's hard to let go when
fear lurks inside you.*

He tussled with his thoughts about the cherished past, about his deep-water pond the way it was. The memories reached out to him. After all, the pond was the only place he had ever known.

But who can guess that precise moment when your world is going to change, when out of some divine blue, providence provides you with the strength to hold on or to let go. To be awake to choice is to be awake to transformation.

As Ping sat in the stuckness of the mud, pondering his choices, a most important revelation came to him. His life was his to live intentionally.

Ping made the choice to let go of his past, engage the future, and give birth to the great new idea of his life.

It was five minutes before dawn on the seventh day when Ping took a final glance back at his once beloved surroundings, let go all the glories of his past adventures, and made the most perfect leap into the greatest adventure of all. . . .

2

Wise Eyes

Be ever mindful of the Way, paying attention to the seen and the unseen.

Ping seemed almost to fly at the beginning. Feeling positive, energetic, with a renewed expansive spirit, Ping wanted to reach the highest heights, cover the greatest distances, and with determined perseverance, experience all the magnificence of life's wonders.

Those were his intentions, anyway.

As I have already pointed out, Ping's legs were beyond phenomenal. So mighty were his muscles, that his leaping power was unmatched. Few in this world had his stamina, and fewer still his determination to travel to the beyond.

In other words, jumping was never any problem for him, not so long as his legs worked. To underscore the point, on his first day Ping made terrific time, tirelessly covering a tremendous distance.

That was nothing.

On the second day, never once getting out of breath, he traveled twice the distance.

Again, it was nothing.

And such a shame that, back then, the *Guinness Book of World Records* people weren't around to document the third day when, without a single rest, he whipped out another daily distance record by mid-afternoon.

Once again, it was all for nothing. Because even though Ping had bested himself each day, he ended up delivering himself instead smack into a nightmare.

And what a terrible thing that was.

Now if Ping had known about the thicker-than-you-can-imagine tangle of towering trees that soon surrounded him, he might have stayed home, trapped by his initial doubts.

And if he had known that in the dark wood of reality there is no clear path to openness, he definitely would have stayed at home.

If only.

Ping took a deep breath. Another. Deeper. Bracing himself, body at the ready, he set to work.

Not easy.

He tried with all his might to overcome the thicket of cypress and pine. He jumped and he bounded, each time readjusting his trajectory, going this way, that way, left and right. And no matter where else he elsed, it was all struggle and strife.

Even an unusually strong tailwind was no help—nothing was of any help. Ping did his best. Despite his every attempt, it was no contest.

The sky-topping trees beat him back, pummeling him, brutalizing his body, forcing him to fall like a stone, fast and hard, to the earth. With repeated efforts came cramping in his legs and that didn't help much either.

On this day of days, Ping experienced the world like he had never experienced it before—a world of failure and setback, unkind and uncaring. What a crusher.

Exhausted, Ping sat pale and shaking. He had never been more miserable.

Glazed over with fatigue, he managed to blink away his tears and sighed. He took a final glance at his predicament and, in the very bright moonlight, looked pleadingly up to the heavens for help.

There wasn't any.

Ping sagged; his heart was shredded.

He felt defeated and disheartened, a sad, inept creature, doomed to a miserable life with no possibility for tomorrow, and that, quite simply, was that.

Ping lay devastated on the ground. What a mistake it had been to think he could pursue a life that mattered. He had undertaken this journey with such hopes. He had come so far, tried so hard, but now his great shining dream began to fade.

Who did he think he was? Who was he to think he was so special? Who was he to think that he had what it takes to follow his dream? Who was he to think he possessed the abilities to get what he wanted out of life?

Who—who . . .

The words reverberated, filling Ping's ears. He blinked and did his best to block out the horridness of it all.

Who—who . . .

Again.

Who—who . . .

Then again . . . and continuing.

Now it's probably safe to say there are limits to what a frog's psyche can endure, and to prove the point, Ping, feeling himself starting to go mad, frantically ordered his brain to halt this unrelenting questioning, commanding his gray cells to just STOPPPP!!!!!!!

No use. The dreaded repetition did not lessen.

Who—who . . .

Ping could find no way to hide from this echoing torment.

And with good reason.

If the path you travel has no obstacles,
it leads nowhere.

Ping tilted his head and realized, suddenly, that the repeating taunt of whos were not really whos at all. As Ping paid closer attention, they sounded clearly like whoooooo, whoooooo.

And then Ping understood they were not coming from him. No, they sounded like they were coming out of the chill darkness, from somewhere behind and from above!

Which they were.

"Who—who has not yet discovered the Way will not find it."

Ping pivoted and squinted up into the moonlight.

There, in a giant twisted tree, amidst the sheltering branches, deep in the deepest shadow, blinked a pair of bright, saucer yellow eyes.

Ping looked closer and was relieved. He didn't know a lot of things, but he did know an owl when he saw one.

"My way is blocked. It's the trees that keep me down," Ping blurted defensively.

"The trees that keep you down are the trees

that lift me high. Are they not the same trees?" asked Owl.

"What does that matter?" asked Ping, sounding a bit irritated. "They're keeping me from continuing on my way."

"If the path you travel has no obstacles, it leads nowhere."

Ping didn't have much to say to that.

"How blind you are to the Way," intoned Owl. "The Way is not a path; it is the landscape of the soul that the universe fills with its breath. Within you and without you, it is there for you. Be open to this, and the universe will always lift you up, not keep you down. All else is futile struggle."

Interesting, Ping thought. There was no denying the fact that this owl was one smart old bird. If Owl could help him out, that would be something.

"Can you see where I need to go from up there?" Ping asked.

Headshake from Owl. "To see where you need to go, you need only to go inside yourself, clearing away the confusion of your mind so that it can hear the promptings of your own heart.

"To know who you really are and how you wish to be is the kind of vision even the sightless possess."

"I could use eyes like yours," Ping said. "Would you help me?"

"You must find your own way," said Owl.

There was a weariness to Owl's voice, but also a note of compassion.

"Only your own heart has the power to guide you," Owl continued. "You must rely on yourself over any other offering. Born of the heart, hewn by the spirit, the path to the magic life cannot be taught—it must be taken."

"So where do I begin?" Ping asked.

"Begin where you are," Owl explained. "Start by awakening the Way within. You must become open to the Way in order to receive it."

"How?" Ping wondered.

"Not how," Owl quickly responded, "Now!" And with that, Owl fluttered down from his branch to a perch in front of Ping, ruffled his wings, and smoothed a few feathers with his beak.

"The dream does not begin unless you do," Owl said. "Now is the moment to grasp our existence.

"Too many wait for just the right time and just the right place to act. The very act of waiting actually pushes the desired events away. You must do in order to be."

Ping, naturally, knew none of this. "Please, I need your guidance to get to where I'm going."

"Do you know where it is that you are going? Ultimately?"

Ping pretended to clear his throat. "Sort of."

"If you don't know where you're going, any road will take you there."

Owl took a few steps before turning. Despite his advanced years, Owl moved with a graceful liveliness. He looked at Ping with slight curiosity.

"But to know what you don't know is the

start of everything. This is the start of an intentional life."

"An intentional life?"

"Intentional living means what you do is one with what you are. Clarity of purpose, an open heart, and a lively mind gives us the power to direct our destinies. To live by choice not by chance, this is what it is to live an intentional life."

"Then living an intentional life is what I dream to do!"

"Prepare for disappointment," said Owl.

"You are so obviously wise and great," said Ping. "I ask for your tutelage, please."

"I think not."

"But I have come so far."

"I wish you safe travel back."

"What will I do?"

"Chalk it up to experience. Good luck."

"Again, I ask for your guidance, please."

"Again I tell you, I am sorry. No." And with that Owl flew back up to his branch.

Ping was young, and because of his youthful years, insistence was still very much part of his temperament. Taking no for an answer was simply not something he accepted easily. Irritated, he asked again.

"No."

He beseeched.

"No."

Then he implored.

"No."

Pleaded.

"No."

Sniveled.

"No."

Groveled.

"No."

Begged.

"No."

Then he held his breath and began to jump up and down. Not in frustration, as you might think. What Ping was actually attempting to do, with all of his energies, was to jump up to the branch where Owl was perched. Never mind that his arms and legs were dead tired, Ping was not giving in.

Each jump got him a little higher, a little closer. Who knows where his newfound strength was coming from. Whatever it was, there was no doubt that after a few hours, Ping was killing the air. No veering this time, every jump was getting him just a tad higher.

And that was how it went for much of the night: Ping was constantly jumping, not giving up, trying to plant himself on Owl's branch.

Owl paid no attention, busying himself from time to time with some feather maintenance, until after one final, enormous jump, like lost magic, Ping actually shared the same branch with Owl!

"Attitude equals altitude," said Owl.

"What?"

"Hmmm ... Exactly."

Owl flew down to the mist-shrouded ground. Ping, gasping for breath from his labors, jumped down after him.

"This is fun," he said, panting his lungs out, trying for a joke. "Haven't been able to do much jumping since I arrived here."

Attitude equals altitude.

"Persistent you are. I'll grant you that," said Owl.

Ping detected a subtle softening in Owl's attitude. "Well, if being persistent is something that will help me live an intentional life, then that is what I'll do."

"Persistence is the difference between a strong will and a strong won't," Owl replied.

"Then you will teach me?" Ping asked, with mounting excitement.

Owl blinked in his direction. "I prefer to spend my time unpestered, but I am reminded only of this: It is said, 'When the student is ready, the teacher will appear.'"

Ping lit up. He understood happy news when he heard it. It was thrilling not to make the journey alone. "I cannot find the words to thank you."

"Then we're off to a wonderful start because, for now, I would appreciate not even a peep from you. Quiet is what you will need if you are to tap into your passion, your true purpose, your heart."

3

Beginner's Mind

An instant of realization makes its home in a
quiet mind.

And with that piece of advice, off went Owl,
heading down the moonlit path for who-
knows-where, with Ping excitedly trooping
behind, keeping as quiet as he could, his
thoughts going in no particular direction.

For Ping, it was not easy to do any solid
thinking with his stomach gurgling. He had
not eaten for some time, and he wondered if
he should say something to Owl. But he decid-
ed against it, fearing it might upset Owl and
send him flying off for another branch, and
Ping had had enough of that.

So in silence he followed right behind Owl, looking for flying bugs, squirmies, crawlers, or any other nibbles of nourishment, fighting against the beginning throbs of a migraine. It was another hour before Ping finally asked where they were going.

Owl said nothing.

Ping then asked Owl if he would explain things when they got there.

"I'll explain things to you now since you do not want to take advantage of walking with your thoughts."

"Right, right. Sorry," Ping said.

Owl scowled. "Apologies not needed for me. You must pay attention to your own thoughts. Take time to still your mind from all that is around you. Connect with your inner self.

"Beyond words, beyond the chatter of concepts and judgments lies a place beyond place, where the conflicts of the mind are silenced by the true calling of the heart.

"Eventually, you will come to know the true journey of life is the movement of the heart towards its home."

Owl paused by a root-entwined stump and closed his eyes. "Listen. Can you hear it? Can you hear the voice of your heart?

"If not, then go deeper. It is there waiting. Welcome its strength. Learn to trust its inexhaustible power. The moment you hear its call, follow it, for it will always know where to take you."

Ping closed his eyes and attempted to concentrate. It didn't come easily.

"Distraction still pulls you," Owl explained.

"Concentrate on emptiness. Let go of all that you know. You must be empty in order to openly receive the life that is yours. Only when we are empty can we be filled. Then you will find Beginner's Mind.

"But for now, you must practice bringing a total focus to what you do. At first, it will take great energy. Then like all things that are practiced, an ease will develop.

"Learn to become one with the task at hand, and then you become one with the universe and all the abundance that it can provide."

Listen. Can you hear it? Can you hear the voice of your heart?

Ping gazed at Owl with a look of wonder. There was no doubting Owl's wisdom.

Sitting very straight, summoning the silence, Ping began again, with deep and steady concentration.

Owl advised that only in darkness can you see the awakening of the true self.

Ping closed his eyes and into the darkness he went. Not just his soul needed searching, he thought, but his spirit too. And for that matter, his heart as well.

Ping's mind began racing, and he sighed. Clearly it would take many more lessons from Owl to make a difference.

For his part Owl didn't mind. He knew that access to the innate intelligence of the universe was dependent on the truth that it is the learners who survive the learned. As mentor, Owl knew his job was to provide not only instruction, but encouragement and patience.

So began the lessons.

For weeks, Owl instructed Ping on a world of things, starting with the significance of risk-taking—not the throw-caution-to-the-wind kind that leads far too many to failure, but the well-planned, calculated-action kind that promises a strong possibility of success.

Owl explained that in order to experience wonder you have to experience the taking of risks. Risk converts opportunity into reality.

However, Owl was very careful to warn Ping about the importance of clearly under-standing the consequences that accompany risk-taking.

"A risk well defined is already a risk half-taken," Owl said.

"Clarify the risk. Define it in precise terms. Determine what obstacles and difficulties you will have to overcome in order to succeed.

"Prepare for contingencies. What is the worst-case scenario? What is your fall-back plan? In other very important words: Look before you leap!"

(Aside: I have it from an unimpeachable source that this very conversation was the ori-gin of the age-old adage.)

Ping took the whole business very much to heart, committing it all to memory, especially the statement that Owl paused to make such a point of: "To avoid taking a risk is to take the biggest risk of all."

Right then and right there, Owl explained that only those who risk something have the ability to achieve something, and that so often the path to success is the one most often not taken.

"Become a purveyor of possibility," Owl urged. "Know that mistakes can be overcome but inaction imprisons the soul.

"Remember, you will always be more disappointed by the things that you didn't do than by the things that you did. Again, you must do in order to be."

And as Ping asked question after question, Owl went to great lengths to underscore how risk is the catalyst for transformation that can transport you from where you are to where you want to be.

To grow is to risk. A failure to take risks will result in failure to experience your destiny.

Summing up, Owl stressed the import of studying risk from all angles, trumpeting,

"The best angle from which to approach risk-taking is from the try angle."

Ping understood, and made the following pledges:

"I promise to do my best to accept the challenges of risk.

"I will make careful assessments of taking a risk and weigh it against not taking a risk.

"I will, as you have instructed, make smart risk-taking a part of my life.

"I will build my risk-taking confidence, starting with taking small risks, working my way up until I am comfortable and confident in the taking of larger risks.

"Owl, you are a genius. I promise I will not fail."

"And I promise you that you will fail," Owl was quick to correct. "Often and miserably, more than you can imagine. Each failure will be paralyzingly painful and will make you cringe and cry and give up in a minute, because that is what failure can do.

"But, as devastating and demoralizing as failure is, there is something much more tragic and terribly worse: the absence of failure. For then you have not exerted the will to attempt success.

"Adopt the philosophy that failure is one of nature's wonderful teachers.

"Just as water effortlessly nourishes all things, failure enriches—it imparts truth and wisdom, insight and knowledge that help you grow. Regard failure as teachings, nothing more, nothing less.

"What you must hold close is this: Do not allow failure to keep you from your wants or desires and prevent you from living a life well lived.

"Failure can be defeating or defeated. Alas, it will always be up to you."

"I'm no quitter," Ping said.

"We'll see," Owl said, quietly to himself.

4

The Test

The true way is burning desire, for the purest metal is the result of the hottest fire.

Now was the time for Owl to give Ping a small task to test his character and courage.

"I know you think you're good at jumping," Owl said, "but let me see how good you are at getting up and walking around a bit."

Ping shook his head. "I couldn't quite make out what you said."

"I am old and sometimes my wings are stiff and ache with arthritis, but my speech is clear. You heard me."

Ping stared at Owl incredulously. "Forgive

me, but in the first place, I can't walk. I have never walked before.

"And in the second place, I'm not the greatest jumper on the planet for nothing. Whatever the destination might be, jumping is all that I will ever need to get me where I go."

Owl glared and bellowed back, "Now pay very strict attention. Walk you can and walk you will, beginning now, or it's been most fascinating spending this time together and I wish you joyous jumping to wherever such a singular talent takes you. I'm sure you will do just fine."

Ping turned pale. Owl's dismissal speech was not lost on him. If he didn't at least attempt to follow Owl's direction, Owl's masterful mentoring would be over for him, and with it would go everything he wanted and needed. That much he knew.

Now, for the past one hundred and fifty years or so, a bit of a battle has been waged among some in the scientific community as to whether frogs possess the ability to walk.

Herpetology honchos are quick to argue

that the African walking frog that resides on the western coast of Ecuador and the North American green tree frog both prefer walking to jumping. The naturalist folks, who are famous for not backing down from a dispute, claim that what is really going on with these two species is more of a crawling movement. Semantics aside, if you're looking for the ultimate proof that a frog can get up on its hind legs and set out for a stroll, you should have been there that one particular nightfall to see Ping do just exactly that.

But not the first time.

Not the second time either.

And if you had some place to go that evening, you probably would have gone, since waiting around for Ping to actually take a few serious steps took quite a while. The sight of a discombobulated frog, stumbling, tripping, and falling on his face was not a pretty one.

"I can't do this," agonized Ping.

Owl didn't seem the least bit surprised.

His wise eyes pinned Ping with a stare. "Believe you can't and you won't. Believe you

To be awake to choice is
to be awake to transformation.

can and you will. Words form belief; belief forms action."

Owl continued, "To take control of your destiny, you must take control of your thoughts. How and what you think will determine your future.

"When it comes to living your dream, whether you think you will or think you won't, you're right either way. If you would like, I will share with you a helpful insight to keep you up and going."

Ping pleaded, "Tell me, please. My knees are scraped and I'm teetering here, about to go sprawling down again, so what's the secret?"

There was a pause, and then Owl whispered these exact words: "To live an intentional life, do not walk on your legs but on your will."

Ping reflected for a moment, marveling at Owl's smartness. How lucky it was for him to come upon such a teacher. Ping realized that he could not disappoint him.

Filled with renewed confidence, he entered a state of deep focused concentration, regained his steadiness, then, with head held back, took a deep breath and, with all the power of will he could muster, tried one step forward.

And fell again.

Hard.

Total-wipeout disaster.

Pathetic.

"I could use another hint here."

"Fall down seven times, stand up eight," Owl advised.

"Be one-hearted and one-minded.

"Living an intentional life is a step-by-step process, in which each step forward brings you closer to the realization of the greatness that lies within.

"Accept this and you take the first step."

Determined, Ping followed Owl's words, trying again and again, until at last the fates smiled, and suddenly there he was, his amazing legs taking one step, then a second step, a third step, a fourth great step, then a few more, his balance becoming established.

Ping had no idea where his new ability was coming from, but here he was putting one leg in front of the other—moving along as if it were nothing new. Even Owl could not deny what a startling spectacle it was to see a frog plodding along upright, but that wasn't the point.

The point was that Ping had had the courage to take a risk, fail, try again and again, and finally succeed. Ping was indeed walking, but the crazy fact was that it was his faith in himself that had him floating above the ground.

"Look at me!"

Owl watched him calmly. "You overcame doubt by leaving it behind. Skepticism has lost its grip on you.

"Never forget that faith in yourself must be a part of your every action and thought. This will sustain you against setbacks and defeats.

"But know, too, that no matter how great your faith in your talent and your skill, you will wander the world aimlessly if you don't have a true vision."

"Hmmm...interesting." Ping shrugged. "Maybe if the moon was a bit brighter, I could see a bit truer."

Owl could only shake his head. "Your vision is your higher wisdom. It is higher wisdom that clears your path.

"Once again I tell you to take the time to awaken your mind, your heart, and your spirit to the echo of your life's destiny. Listen to the silences between the sounds—this is the music of your soul.

"There are always two journeys you must take to discover the Way: one to lose yourself and one to find yourself.

"Exhaust words.

"There is nothing that is outside the mind. You must look inward before you can move outward on your journey."

Ping thought he understood and beamed. "I don't mind so much taking a few moments to come up with something."

Owl stared at the heavens and sighed. Deeply. Then he flew above to a tree branch and got comfortable, the sun beginning to rise on the horizon.

Still, Owl was an eternal optimist and thought this was a lesson that Ping would not have to linger on for long. Maybe the next few months would be enough ... and then again it might take a little longer than that.

5

Visionary Quest

Listen to the voice of the cedars when no wind stirs. There you will find yourself.

The winter winds came early. The icy bluster scattered the plum leaves across the ground and swayed the needles of the ancient pines. Over six months had passed since Ping left his native pond.

Now, Ping sat hunkered in a dark, dank log hollow. Pinched with cold, he heard the clacking of the bamboo grove, but his mind was not there. Hadn't been for weeks. He had sent it away to somewhere beyond form and sound to a place of astonishing beauty and being.

Ping had found himself, finally and at last,

in the inner landscape of a settled mind. Owl had shown him the Way through meditation.

This was a different frog. Every morning Ping would sit in inner quiet for hours.

On this particular morning, he was deep in meditation as usual. Then, in his mind's eye, he had this purifying vision: In the distance, soaring snow-capped mountain peaks sparkled in the dancing spring sun. The wonderfully warming rays were melting the snow, filling the streams and pools of the garden with waters clear and deep. And not even the most articulate of frogs could ever hope to describe the sights and scents of the blooming magnolias and cherry blossoms that scattered their petals and perfumed the air, or the lovely colors of the flowering wisteria, azaleas, and irises on display at the moss-laden pondside.

Still enjoying this magnificent inner vision, Ping savored the joyful soundscapes: the choir of birdsong and the gentle babbling of water interrupted only by the splashes coming from young, jubilant frogs trying their best to go the distance.

Ping's heart was full. He was in a place few of us are ever fortunate enough to visit: He was momentarily living inside his vision.

Later that day Ping described his vision to Owl. "Is it possible that such a place of bliss and splendor exists here on Earth?" he asked.

Owl nodded that such a wonder of the world did in fact exist. "There is a place called the Emperor's Garden that ranks among the treasures on Earth. It is a place of bliss and greatest splendor just like the place in your vision. But to savor its exalted grandeur, you will have to travel many miles, fraught with many challenges."

Owl informed Ping that the greatest cause for trembling would be the necessity to cross Splat River.

"But this is my destiny," Ping quickly responded.

Now in my desire to present this story with the utmost accuracy, I need to point out that for centuries Splat River has been officially mapped by cartographers as Rock River, but was called Splat River by the local inhabitants of the woods who witnessed so many travelers go *splat* when they tried to cross the treacherous waters.

The river's swift, smashing currents and jagged rocks were deadly. Local denizens knew better than to even think about attempting to cross Splat River. Whatever reason one had for getting to the other side was not important enough to doom one's life.

"Not a problem," Ping stated, unafraid. "You've never seen how far I can jump. Just show me this Splat River and I'll show you how I can get across without even dunking a toe. That's how great my talent is when it comes to jumping—such is my skill."

"What is foolishly thought may foolishly be dared," Owl said.

"I don't understand," said Ping.

"You're about to," said Owl. "Talent comes naturally, while skill must be learned.

"I have seen your talents with my own eyes, but talents are incomplete when not aligned with skills. Talent may open doors, but skill will allow you to go through.

"You must develop both talent and skill, or you will never be a master of your life."

Ping sat silent for moment. Blinked. Blinked again. "I want to become master of my life."

"To want is not enough. There is only to do. You must do in order to master the circumstances of life, or risk having the circumstances of life master you."

"I am ready."

"Then we begin," announced Owl.

And so they did in earnest.

The training schedule was simple. Undeviating. No frills. It began by building Ping's muscles, making them strong enough to face the challenge of Splat River.

Ping started his exercises by holding one-pound rocks in his fingers while hanging upside down from a tree branch for a half an hour every day. At first this caused him trouble, and although his arms ached and his legs hurt, he kept at it.

Within a month, Ping could hold five-pound rocks. And while the blood rushing to an upside-down head would mean headaches

*Talent comes naturally, while
skill must be learned.*

for most, Ping got to the point where he would seldom pass a branch without grabbing a couple of rocks to happily get in some extra upside-down time.

Then to build up his thighs, for three hours every day, Ping would do log lifts, similar to what we call leg lifts. He would balance a heavy log on his feet, lifting it in the air, pushing it up and down with his legs while lying on his back.

For further strength and stamina, he spent three more hours each day on jumping jacks and squat jumps, followed by jumping from above and from below, whipping out jumps in all directions, umpty-umpth jumps each week, so that the very act of jumping would always come without a second thought.

Owl explained the difference between natural skill and being skillful, that training leads to technique, which in turn leads to talent and skill becoming one total embodiment, always instinctive and immediate.

This is how training went for Ping, hour

after hour, grabbing forty winks only whenever he could.

Ping's practice sessions continued day after day, until there had been a whole year of this concerted effort.

While days were spent strengthening the body, nights were spent strengthening Ping's mind, because there were still many mysteries that needed solving.

Some of these mysteries had to do with the universe, but most had to do with Ping's golden place in it.

Owl explained: "The unknown is always. Never count on the future, nor your ability to control it. To live an intentional life is to recognize yourself as being one with the process of the present.

"Change is a constant companion, allowing for the limitless possibilities that it holds for all living things.

"Have the grace to make the universe your partner, welcoming the opportunities that are the result of continuing change.

"Go with the flow, and you will find yourself supported by the mysterious unity of its power.

"When change comes to visit, when obstacles come into view, be as what you are from: Be as water."

"I will be all that I can be," Ping replied.

"No, be more of what you are."

"You needn't worry," was Ping's answer. "Thanks to your teachings I have the power to swim upstream if I ever have to."

Recent months had taught Owl that Ping was a good learner, but not a particularly fast one.

Owl continued: "To possess the power of true strength is to possess the ability to yield, to change course if need be.

"Again I instruct you to be as if water. Few elements are more yielding than water—it is the softest most yielding thing, yet its power is such that it can ultimately prevail over hardest rock or the strongest steel. Fluid and flexible, water twists and turns, flowing around, over, under—it changes its direction freely along the way.

"There is nothing that water cannot overcome, yet its essential nature is to yield, to give way.

"Water has the relentless power to transform and restructure all things that stand in its path. As do you.

"Know that you have the capacity to greet uninvited obstacles with a mindful flow, changing jeopardy, problems, and challenges into opportunities, defeat into victory."

Ping was confused. "Let me get this straight. I use this flow to figure out what I need to do?"

Owl replied, "Other voices will try to lead you to what you need to do, the flow will lead you to what needs to be done.

"The flow is your natural path, the force that allows you to persevere against inner doubts and external adversities.

"The flow is everywhere. It is the movement of all life. It has no beginning and has no end. The flow is the total ongoing process of the universe.

"Go with the flow, because the flow knows

where to go. Align your daily life with it and you will ride its boundless wave, taking advantage of its all-knowing direction. Abandon its way, and you abandon your right to live life to the fullest.

"To live an intentional life is to enter the stream of your destiny, always making use of its current."

"It's a strange thing," said Ping. "I feel as if I have learned so much and at the same time I feel as if I have learned nothing."

Owl said, "There are no words to contain all wisdom. Such is true enlightenment. What you mean is that you are ready to seek your destiny. Just as I believe that you are."

"Yes, that's what I mean," answered Ping.

Then Owl did the most remarkable and unexpected thing. He bowed and, in a very, very quiet voice, said, "To do is to be."

And with that, Owl turned and headed down the seldom-traveled path that led to Splat River. Ping jumped right behind, a much humbler and wiser frog than he was when he first entered these woods many months ago.

6

Current Event

The sage embraces the one and becomes the model for all.

White noise.

Louder and louder white noise. That's what greeted Owl and Ping when they approached the sheer cliff walls that fell away, down to Splat River. The foaming power of rushing rapids and twisting currents roared, pounding the rocks, a constant thunder rising up to the heavens.

The perfect light of the full moon brightened the scene. Ping hopped onto a boulder and surveyed the river's force.

It was dizzying. There was a sudden pressure in his heart. In this contemplative moment he began to feel a twinge of uncertainty but would not allow it to surface.

"Such is the challenge," from Owl.

"Pollywog play," from Ping, with a drop of doubt in his voice.

Then nothing from either as the silence between them almost matched the constant, booming waters of Splat River.

A sudden shining began to pool in Ping's eyes. There was so much he wanted to say, but wondered how and where to begin.

Ping didn't have to wonder long. Owl sensed it all and made a sweeping gesture with his right wing.

He gazed at the treacherous waters. "A river has no shape," he said. "It is only contained by the boundaries it carves out for itself. You too are like the river."

"I hope I have what it takes," Ping responded.

Owl turned to Ping, facing him directly. Quietly he intoned: "To live an intentional life, belief and will are what it takes. With these two things, all is possible.

"The way is not in the sky, the way is in the heart. For the traveler who knows his direction, there is always a favorable wind."

"Thank you for the lessons learned," Ping said humbly.

Owl said: "It is not what you have learned, but what you do with it that will create your difference. You can fulfill your destiny by helping others.

"A thousand candles can be lit from a single candle. Be a giver of light. Use your capacity to inspire and uplift others."

"I will tell my story to everyone I meet," Ping affirmed.

"Those who live an intentional life do not tell their story. By example, they are the story. You must do in order to be. Go thrill the world."

Ping gave a soft nod of his head. "You just watch me."

"This I will." And with those words, Owl took flight until he reached a perfect observation point, hovering two hundred and fifty feet above, centered over Splat River. Waiting.

Ping blinked and blinked again as he stared

*A risk well defined is already
a risk half-taken.*

down at the water's intense churn. Then he loosened the muscles in his neck, rocking his head left, then right, and stretched his legs as he began to concentrate.

He had to consider every detail if he was going to successfully cross Splat River to reach the other side. He had to account for the wind's speed and direction and combine that with what he knew about trajectory.

Ping evaluated and calculated and considered.

He approximated and analyzed and surmised.

For, yes, he had to concern himself with angle and distance, and true, he had to assess the height, and, absolutely, of course, he had to gauge for gravity—all of these things had to be factored into flight or down he would go, so his mind spun, moving in a whir.

Then, amidst it all, a most truly amazing thing happened.

His mind went empty.

Blank.

Vacant.

Clear.

His mind was void of any inhibition or doubt, and was filled with only a sense of oneness with the air.

In sum, Ping was about to become one with the experience.

Ping looked down, then across, and flashed one final smile up to Owl.

Then he took one final deep breath for courage. Embued with the power of will and belief and intention, he jumped just the highest jump he had ever jumped, with an arc of such perfection that left no doubt he would clear Splat River with plenty to spare.

"Fly!" Owl yelled, and, indeed, Ping flew farther and farther, soaring through the air with remarkable grace, conquering the expanse between the banks with singular ease.

There was no thought about any of this because Ping's mind was clear, his oneness with the air carrying him farther than he had ever gone before.

Oh, what pride Owl must have felt as he saw Ping defy all laws of gravity, but Owl felt and saw nothing.

Not the rush of wings that came from above, straight and deadly.

Not the size of the huge hawk that swooped down without warning.

Not until the hawk's razor-sharp talons sheared into the muscles of the old Owl's back did he feel anything, and that only for an instant.

7

The Flow

A river flows to join the spiraling dance of life.

The explosion of feathers burst the air, breaking Ping's perfect concentration.

"Noooooooo!" Ping screamed as he saw the hawk fly away with Owl in his grasp. Just a few feathers zigzagging downward were all that remained of Owl.

Ping went spiraling wildly out of control, plunging, windmilling end over end, down and down still more, with nothing below to break his fall, nothing but the rapids and the rocks of Splat River.

Which, within a finger snap, had him.

Totally.

As Ping plummeted into the rushing rapids, he wildly kicked at the icy water. He was stunned that his mighty legs were no match for the even more mighty, teeming, white-water torrents that were sweeping him away.

Ping struggled madly. He sank and surfaced, sank and surfaced again and again, yanked under the water for a second, the next moment pushed under for an eternity.

Still he kicked harder and harder, thinking that he would rise enough to find a way to gain control, go against the current, and swim to the safety of shore.

His once tireless legs began to flail feebly, his strength began to leave him, his whole world began to leave him. Belief was every-thing, and Ping's was going, going so fast.

Now he could only use his weakening arms to fend off the rocks that were bashing his body.

There was nothing that Ping could do to stop the painful punishment—the more he tried to fight against the breakers, the more the roaring surge slammed him against the rocks, pummeling him, gashing his skin, and tattering his soul.

Ping's feeble attempts to conquer the current seemed all too little. Splat River would have none of it, its cresting rush had its hold on him, attacking him, shooting him through swirls, smashing him hard against boulder jags.

Exhausted, he panicked badly, losing his buoyancy, yet with every ounce of strength remaining, he tried to kick, to grab, to somehow escape the fate that now seemed inevitable.

Zero chance.

Ping's world went white behind his eyes. Splat River began to claim him. He started to sink. Doom was only seconds away.

Then somehow, by some miracle, he remembered Owl's words.

"Be as you are . . . Be as if water."

Not a lot of words, but enough.

Suddenly, salvation seemed possible.

Ping remembered Owl's teachings, giving himself over to them.

"Fluid and flexible, water twists and turns, flowing around, over, under—it changes its direction freely along the way, overcoming obstacles," Owl had said.

"To live an intentional life is to learn how to swim with an existence that flows. Go with the flow, because the flow knows where to go."

Ping started to do that very thing, startled at first, by how swiftly the water loosened its death grip and instead supported him, guided him, protected him, as it simply followed its own nature around the rocks and boulders.

More fascinating still was the remarkable power Ping began to feel as he adapted to the flow, befriending it, dancing with it, on and on. By doing so he was becoming an agent of change himself, feeling the rightness of it.

This wonderful moment revealed that living an intentional life was simply to let the potential of his life live through him.

How true.

As Owl had told him, "Happiness is not a destination. It is a process, a wondrous, winding journey."

He could hear Owl's voice saying, "Following the flow is a way of life that sustains us, guides us, and leads us to boundless joy and insight."

Life, after all, is for us to live, fully, wonderfully.

We are travelers, journeying together, each and all created to live glorious lives that matter, allowing for our truest destiny to take its course.

And since time is like a river, how long Ping traveled down the great watercourse of Splat River, how many more minutes, hours, days, weeks, maybe months had passed before it delivered him to his destiny is unclear. There is no time frame for how long one must spend waiting for happiness.

It's just not necessary.

Ping had learned this one simple essential truth: While we spend our time waiting for happiness, happiness is always here waiting for us.

Happiness is the great core of our reality, rooted within, ready to be deservedly claimed.

*Go with the flow, because
the flow knows where to go.*

The Flow

Within each of us there is a Ping, for we are not born into the world but born out of it. (And certainly Owl lives on in Ping through his teachings.)

When we follow our nature, we give full expression to our souls, our talents, our gifts, our passion, our power, our deepest sense of who we are and how we wish to be.

When we flow in complete accord with our correct path, a lot of wonderful truths suddenly become evident.

Our joy—the magical life—was with us all along, waiting only to be recognized for the fundamental force it is.

Can we really live a life that is both ageless and timeless?

Bet on it.

And for those of you who are still wondering about how long it was before Ping discovered his bliss, you would not be amiss for wanting to know. So let me just say, quietly:

For all the time it took . . . it took no time at all.

Epilogue

I read a lot.

Unfortunately, not as much as I would like for all kinds of reasons: It's way too hard between the many demands of work, the shifting needs of a growing family, plus the innumerable invitations to lecture and all the other pure pleasure perks that are a result of helping guide a thriving business and writing books. But still I wake up every morning of the world to pore over as much as I can, reading the reports that I must, carefully choosing other great material of interest.

I mostly sneak in the less serious stuff whenever I'm traveling, taking a break from burdening my brain with commerce, usually staying clear of the business tomes. I make it a point to happily clock the time in a packed plane with a wellspring of general interest books, magazines, journals, and papers, just to remind myself what the Grail is like.

Why am I telling you all this?

It was on one of my travels, skying from the left coast to the right coast in an airliner at some thirty-seven thousand feet when I came across a just so dazzlingly wonderful article in that day's paper that locked my total attention. This is exactly how the headline read:

NEW FROG JUMPS THOUSANDS OF YEARS.
REMARKABLE DISCOVERY EXCITES SCIENTISTS.

Yes, you read that right, and here is the gist of the story as it was printed:

An ecological treasure of a new frog species has been discovered among the lush, serene wetlands of China's Imperial Garden. Located on the north-western outskirts of Beijing and revered for its architectural grandeur, landscaped beauty, and pristine ponds, the Imperial Garden has also been known as "the garden of gardens" by the Chinese for centuries.

The discovery of this unique species makes the wetlands a new center of frog diversity and increases the urgency for protecting the area of habitat from the effects of mass development.

Biologists at the Free University of Brussels in Belgium described the new species as so remark-able for its powerful hind legs and jumping ability

that it warrants the establishment of a new frog
family, of which it is the only member.

I was stunned.

Excited, too, as I went with the hoopla of the article, each sentence tugging on my heartstrings,
reconfirming my belief that happiness is, indeed, in
the air we breathe, a constant that awaits us all. By
the time I got back to my office, so keyed up was I
with anticipation, hoping happily that Google might
possibly have more of the story, that I went to my
computer first thing. Harried.

And you know what? I almost fell out of my chair
when I was able to pull up a picture of the new frog
find.

Even today, if you do a search, study the picture
you hit upon, and see the blithe, happy smile, you
will not doubt its ancestry. And as exhilarating as
the whole thing is, the article noted that because of
environmental problems, the future of this new
species may be in dire doubt.

Maybe they're right.

Maybe.

Me, I'll go with Owl's words: To change the
future, one needs only to change the present, and
that anyone's real future begins with a triumphant
commitment to the present.

As for the past, well that, as you have hopefully come to know now ... is another story.

Wishing you a leaping love-what-you-do, do-what-you-love life.

Acknowledgments

Within each of us, there are stories: the kind of wonderful stories that can make our lives and the lives around us better—stories that provide memories that gladden us and bring a smile or sadden us with a tear, terrific stories that can open the intellect, wondrous stories waiting to leap out if only we would let them. Now more than ever I believe that stories can bring us through the rapids and make us a better society, a better people, and a better world. When something wonderful manages to be told, magic happens.

This book would not be if it wasn't for the rich contributions of others, people who have listened to my stories and who have shared theirs with me. Hats off to them all: especially to Machiko for her touching and brilliantly done brushstrokes of Ping; to my unerring barometer of an editor, Keith Hollaman; to Heidi Sachner for her instinct on what's important; to Harry Burton, Mary Williams, Fauzia Burke, and John Burke for taking it from the pond to the street; to Kevin McGuinness and Jerry Pfeifer for their visual acuity and to Paul Sugarman and Frank DeMaio for putting it all together. Finally and importantly: to my publisher, Esther Margolis, whose encouragement and guidance help me find water in the desert.

About the Author

Stuart Avery Gold is a zentrepreneur, author, future-finder, and both imagineer and champion of imagineers. Stuart is the former chief operating officer of The Republic of Tea and is recognized as one of the innovative gurus behind the success of the Novato, California–based company. Stuart oversaw the company's brand building, marketing, and product development strategies.

Stuart is coauthor with Ron Rubin, owner and board chairman of The Republic of Tea, of the Zentrepreneur Guides® series of books, including *Success at Life; Dragon Spirit; Tiger Heart, Tiger Mind; Wowisms;* and *The Zentrepreneur's Idea Log and Workbook.* Translated into languages around the world, the books have been lauded by Tom Peters, Seth Godin, Al and Laura Ries, Jeffrey Fox, Cheryl Richardson, and Melinda Davis, and described by *Newsweek* as "a blend of business advice and spiritual teachings for the 21st century."

Stuart currently consults with entrepreneurs and corporations and writes and speaks about success strategies for personal and business empowerment. He has lectured at numerous schools including the Wharton School of Business, the New School, and Parsons School of Design, and at Fortune 500 companies, including American Express.

Stuart is based in Boca Raton, Florida, and can be reached at the website www.pingthebook.com or by e-mail at info@stuartaverygold.com.

SHARE THE JOURNEY

Ping is a story of celebration that honors the past, energizes the present, and can profoundly shape the direction of your future by giving you the insights to help deal with life's daily challenges and changes effectively. Like some of the mythical heroes of old, Ping is a hero for all times, a metaphor for whatever you want in your life, a liberating invitation that urges you to see beyond your existing horizons of the familiar and comfortable into a new and more exciting way of living, by realizing your true nature and never-ending potential.

Tell us your story

As the proud publisher of this book, we hope that *Ping* has inspired you to make a leap at life's possibilities. The fact that you purchased this book proves that you are open to your limitless potential. If someone gave you this book, it proves that someone recognizes your limitless potential. The author and we invite you to share your thoughts and experiences about *Ping* and to tell us your story by contacting us at ping@newmarketpress.com